GARDEN OF THE GODS, PIKES PEAK
COLORADO

by
Bob D'Antonio

Chockstone Press
Evergreen, Colorado
1996

Classic Rock Climbs: Garden of the Gods, Pikes Peak, Colorado

Cover photo by Stewart Green, Ed Webster in Garden of the Gods.

ISBN: 1-57540-025-1 *Classic Rock Climbs* series
1-57540-027-8 *Garden of the Gods, Pikes Peak, Colorado*

Published and distributed by:
Chockstone Press, Inc.
Post Office Box 3505
Evergreen, CO 80437-3505

DEDICATION

This book is dedicated to my mother, Judy D'Antonio. Her love, support and sense of adventure have been with me through all my endeavors.

ACKNOWLEDGMENTS

A book of this scope would not be possible without the help of many people. First, I'd like to thank my best friend and wife of 21 years, Laurel. Without her support and understanding of my love for climbing, none of my climbing dreams would have come true.

Most of these areas hold a special place in my climbing heart, I lived in the Colorado Springs area for seven years and have many fond memories of climbing in the Garden, Elevenmile Canyon, Pike's Peak and Mueller State Park. Thanks to Richard Aschert, Lew Hoffman, Bob Robertson, Larry Kledzik, Chuck Carlson, Stewart Green and all the other partners I had the pleasure to climb with.

Thanks to all the climbers who gave me information, comments and proofread parts of the manuscript, including Stewart Green, Mark Milligan, Mark Van Horn, Dave Dangle, Mark Rolofson, Steve Cheyney, Kerry Gunter, Richard Aschert, Bob Robertson, Peter Gallagher and Glen Schuler. A big special thanks to my friend Jon Hardy for the use of his Powerbook and to Mark Sonnenfeld for all his help and advice that made this project a lot easier. Thank you to Betty Alf for her help on the road maps. Special thanks go to Stewart Green for all his help in proofreading the material for this book, the use of his excellent photos and access to his vast store of knowledge of the area.

GARDEN OF THE GODS, COLORADO. PHOTO: STEWART M. GREEN

TABLE OF CONTENTS

RICHARD ASCHERT ON *POSITIONS AVAILABLE*, TABLE MOUNTAIN. PHOTO BY STEWART M. GREEN.

INTRODUCTION

GARDEN OF THE GODS, PIKES PEAK
COLORADO

The Pikes Peak area of Colorado offers some of the most diverse and accessible technical rock climbing in the United States. From the sandstone towers of the Garden of the Gods, to the pink alpine granite of Pikes Peak, few areas in the country can compare to this place for sheer beauty and abundant rock for the climber to practice his or her craft.

This is a no-frills rock climbing guide to select areas that surround the city of Colorado Springs. Areas included are: Pikes Peak, Garden of the Gods, The Martyr, Table Mountain, Rampart Range Road. This is not a comprehensive guide. It is a select guide and not all routes at all areas are listed.

CLIMBING DANGERS AND SAFETY   Once you put on your climbing shoes or rope up, you run the chance of getting hurt or killed. Some of the routes in this guide are dangerous and should only be attempted by climbers confident in his or her ability to climb at a high level of skill. Don't be fooled by numbers, a 5.9 on a sport route is much easier than a 5.9 at 12,000 ft. on Pikes Peak. If you have done most of your climbing in a gym you should limit your climbing to sport routes. Do not attempt to climb traditional routes without knowing how to place gear and set natural belays.

I have tried to give the most accurate information that I could find to get you to the climbs. Once you are there it is your responsibility to take care of your partner and yourself. If a climb looks too hard, don't do it. If a climb looks too scary, don't do it. Ratings are very subjective and should be taken with a grain of salt. A 5.10 with four bolts in 20 feet is much different from a

MARTHA MORRIS BELAYS
BOB D'ANTONIO ON
MR. FRED (5.10D), GARDEN
OF THE GODS, COLORADO.
PHOTO: STEWART M. GREEN

5.10 with natural gear every 15 feet. If you are just learning how to climb, hook up with a competent guide, you will learn more in one day than you would in weeks on your own.

Self-preservation should always come first. If you are feeling weak, go climb something easy. If you are going to solo a route, do it alone and away from people, they don't want to see your body mangled at the bottom of some cliff. Use common sense. Good judgment can save your life, bad judgment can kill you. This is a guidebook and nothing more. It can't help you climb better, it won't get you up a climb, and it won't minimize the dangers of climbing real rock in the real world.

ETHICS   Most of the climbs in this book were established in the 1970s and '80s. Most of these climbs are traditional climbs, they were done from the ground up with natural gear and bolts that were placed for protection on lead from the ground up. Please respect the accomplishments of the first ascent party. Don't add bolts to established routes, if a bolt needs to be replaced ask the first ascent party's permission. If you want to change the character of a route in any way, ask the first ascent party. Too many people in the Colorado Springs area have taken it upon themselves to change routes without asking. Don't be one of them. If you are trying to do a route and it is too hard, don't alter the route, just work at getting better. A sport route with hard moves and a lot of bolts is just that, hard. A traditional climb with hard moves and difficult gear placements should be left as a testimony to a climber's ability to climb difficult rock in less than ideal conditions.

Chipping and altering routes, especially established routes, not only degrades the first ascent effort, it degrades climbing itself. Most climbers don't care if you hang, grab or fall a hundred times on a route. Climbers do care if you change the route by altering the rock or protection. If the overhanging side of the Spray Wall at Elevenmile Canyon is the future of climbing, with all its chip holds, then personally I think we have none.

In the end, how you ascend a climb is more important than reaching the top. Take pride in how you climb. If you're not up to doing a route in its natural state, don't change the character of a route just to make it easier. Take your frustrations to the rock gym, that's what it is there for. If you find a blank piece of rock, don't chip, look a little harder and you'll find rock with holds on it. What we do today affects what will happens tomorrow. Take pride in how you climb, we are leaving a legacy for other climbers who will come after us. Learn about your sport and read about the history of the areas you are climbing in. Not only will you get a historical perspective, it will enhance your climbing visit. Join the Access Fund and get involved in access issues. Most of all, realize that the rock is not infinite. There is only so much to go around, respect the rock and the privilege that we have of climbing on it.

RATING SYSTEM AND RACK This guide uses the Yosemite Decimal System, the system that most climbers are familiar with. The routes in this book range in difficulty from 5.0 to 5.13. A 5.10 slab route could be easier or harder than a 5.10 crack. Use this system with a grain of salt, some routes at the same grade can be completely different. An R or an X after the grade of a route denotes added danger and one should be competent at or above the level of the climb. An R or X rated climb means that there is little or no protection, and a fall could mean serious injury or death. Remember that all climbs could be R or X rated climbs.

Some routes will have a (+) or (–). This is a subgrade and only means that the route is either easier (–) or harder (+) than a "straight" rating. Just to confuse you a little more, the sub grades of a, b, c, d, are used to rate climbs 5.10 or harder. A 5.10a is usually a lot easier than a 5.10d. Most routes are rated by the most difficult

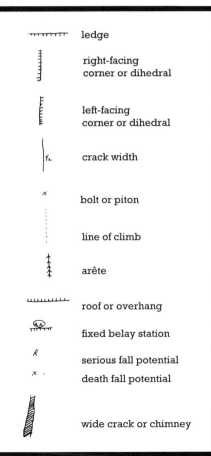

⌐⌐⌐⌐⌐	ledge
	right-facing corner or dihedral
	left-facing corner or dihedral
	crack width
×	bolt or piton
⋮	line of climb
	arête
⌐⌐⌐⌐⌐	roof or overhang
	fixed belay station
R	serious fall potential
× -	death fall potential
	wide crack or chimney

move. A climb with a single move of 5.11 may feel easier than a climb with many moves of 5.10.

A Roman numeral from I to III might follow the technical grade, this indicates the commitment and time factor involved in climbing the route. A Grade I takes a strong party one to two hours to climb, where as a Grade III would or should take a strong party four to five hours to climb. This does not take into account the time walking to and from a climb. An R or a X following the grade means that this route is *serious* and should only be attempted by someone competent at a level above the grade listed.

A one- to three-star rating is included for some routes. This is a personal bias of the author. The star ratings range from one star, indicating good quality, to three stars indicating exceptional quality or historical significance.

A free climbing rack for the routes in this book should include RPs, a set of wired Stoppers, Aliens, TCUs, a set of Friends or other camming devices, eight or so Quickdraws, four runners of various lengths, a few free carabiners, a 165-foot rope and an extra rope for rappels. Having all the gear in the world won't help you if you don't know how to use it. Take the time to gain confidence in your ability to place natural protection.

After all is said and done, it is up to you to respect the rocks and our sport. It is also up to you to bring the proper gear to a climb and scope out the climb before you do it. It is your responsibility to respect the public and private lands that we are permitted to climb on. You should look at climbing as privilege, not just a right. Too many areas have been closed down due to irresponsible climbers, don't be one of the those whose selfish acts hurt the rest of the climbing community.

ACCOMMODATIONS   Colorado Springs is Colorado's second largest city and offers all the benefits of a large city. Campgrounds are limited and family oriented. There are a number of campgrounds located on National Forest lands.There is also the Colorado Springs Youth Hostel, located at 17 North Farragut Avenue that offers warm and comfortable beds at reasonable rates. Restaurants run from Taco Bells to five-star eateries. Good cheap food can be found at a number of restaurants. My favorite places to eat are: La Casita, 1331 S. Nevada; Old Chicago, downtown Colorado Springs; The Manitou Bakery in downtown Manitou Springs; and Poor Richard's Espresso Bar on Boulder and Tejon in downtown Colorado Springs.

WEATHER   Climbing is possible year round at the lower lying crags (Garden, Table Mountain). The climbing season on Pikes Peak usually extends from May to September. The best conditions and stable weather are from March to October. Precipitation, mostly afternoon showers, is likely in June and July.

EMERGENCY SERVICES   In case of emergency contact Colorado Springs Police at 911. Hospitals in Colorado Springs are: Penrose Hospital, 2215 North Cascade, 630-3300 or St. Francis, East Pikes Peak, 473-6830.

MAC JOHNSON BELAYS STEVE HONG ON *DUST TO DUST* (5.10), GARDEN OF THE GODS, 1978. PHOTO: STEWART M. GREEN

GARDEN OF THE GODS, COLORADO.
PHOTO: STEWART M. GREEN

SECTION ONE

GARDEN OF THE GODS

Garden of the Gods, located in the city of Colorado Springs, is one of the most unique climbing areas in the United States. The rocks here are uplifted sandstone hogbacks lying at the base of Pike's Peak. The rock varies in quality from solid edges, huge solution holes and good pockets, to horrifying loose dinner plates and huge blocks ready to fall in your lap all on the same climb. This is not your typical climbing area. The climbs range in height from 40 to 375 feet and from one to five pitches. Most of the climbs are protected with soft, army angle pitons, drilled four to five inches in the soft sandstone. This technique was first used by desert climbing pioneer Harvey Carter. Bear in mind that most of the soft pitons are at least 15 years old, and should be treated with care.

Another unique phenomena of the Garden is the effects of rain and snow on the rock. The rock is soft sandstone and should not be climbed on after periods of heavy moisture. Climbing on the rock when it is wet is not only bad for the rock, but you'll snap off crucial holds, take long falls, scare yourself half to death and ruin the climb for future ascents. Spring snowstorms and summer rainstorms are the most common times for heavy moisture. Winter snowstorms often pose little danger to the rock and should dry out in a matter of days.

Here are some suggestions for climbers coming to the Garden to climb. Don't add any fixed gear to any pre-existing climb. Don't chop any fixed gear on established climbs. Don't create any holds, period! Don't litter, pick up your trash and the trash of others, it won't kill you. Climb clean, leave no visible marks, paint or offensive slings. Use technique, you will have far better success than trying to overpower some soft little sandstone hold. OK, now go have some fun on some of the best soft-sandstone climbing in the world.

CLIMBING HISTORY   The Garden of the Gods is one of the oldest climbing areas in the United States. The great American climbing pioneer Albert Ellingwood was the first person to climb technical routes in the Garden. Considering the soft rock and his crude climbing gear his ascents in the 1920s are nothing short of amazing. With better equipment, in the 1940s, Vernon Twombly and Stanley Boucher climbed several classics including the ever popular Practice Slab on South Gateway Rock. The great desert pioneer, Harvey Carter added a number of hard routes and to this day he is still active in the Pike's Peak area. Carter innovated the use of drilled angles that allowed the opening of some of the more current classics. Climbers from nearby Fort Carson did the first ascents of some moderate classics routes such as *Montezuma's Tower*, *West Point Crack* and the *Three Graces*.

The late 1960s and early 1970s brought on the modern free climbing rage and with it a number of hard free climbs. Jimmy Dunn, Earl Wiggins, Ed Webster and Leonard Coyne were the main activists from this period. Climbs such as *Anaconda*, *Amazing Grace*, *Cocaine* and *Pipe Dreams* were just a few of the great routes done by this group of outstanding climbers. Not only did these climbers add a number of outstanding routes locally, their accomplishments in the world of climbing are mind boggling—Jimmy Dunn's first solo ascent of a new route on El Capitan in Yosemite, Earl Wiggins' ropeless ascent of the *Scenic Cruise* in the Black Canyon in three hours in 1976, Leonard Coyne's first free ascent of the *Forrest-Walker* route (*Stratosfear* 5.11+R/X) in the Black Canyon and Ed Webster's first ascent of a new route on Mount Everest in the Himalayas.

The 1980s brought on a new group of climbers wanting to leave their mark. Bob Robertson, Peter Gallagher, Mark Rolofson, Fred and Richard Aschert, Larry Kledzik and I put up a number of excellent routes. *Cold Turkey*, *Men at Work*, *Horribly Heinous* and *The Refugee* are just some of classic routes from this period. Myself, Richard Aschert and Mark Rolofson were particularly active adding some 50 new routes between them.

The early 1990s brought on a renewed interest in the Garden and with it a few modern sport routes. Ric Geimen and his Ryiobi drill went to work on the east face of Kindergarten Rock and added a number of good routes with *Diesel and Dust* and *Civil Disobedience* being the best. What the future holds for the Garden is hard to predict but there is one thing for sure: the Garden is one the most unusual and beautiful climbing areas in the United States.

I did not include every single route in the Garden. Some routes are not worth doing. This is a personal opinion, aid routes are left out as they offer nothing more than a pull-up on bolts or pins. I have tried to give the visiting climbers the more exceptional, historical and quality routes.

HOW TO GET THERE The Garden of the Gods city park is located on the west side of Colorado Springs. To best access the area, take the Garden of the Gods Road from I-25 and follow the signs or take Ridge Road off US 24.

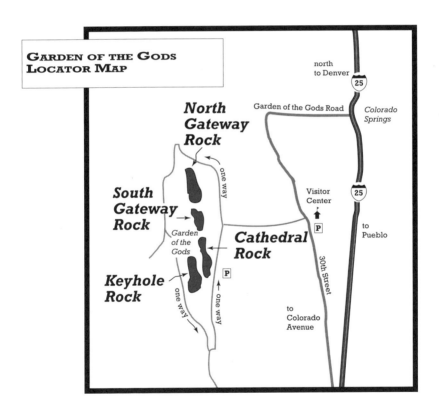

GARDEN OF THE GODS LOCATOR MAP

North Gateway Rock

South Gateway Rock

Keyhole Rock

Cathedral Rock

one way

Garden of the Gods

one way

one way

north to Denver

25

Garden of the Gods Road

Visitor Center

P

30th street

Colorado Springs

25

to Pueblo

to Colorado Avenue

NORTH GATEWAY ROCK

With west-facing exposure, routes up to six pitches long and some of the best rock in the Garden, the climbing on this rock should not be missed. Descent Routes: There are two major descent routes off North Gateway Rock. The Tourist Gully runs the length of the Finger Face and offers easy access on and off the routes on the face. The city of Colorado Springs installed huge eyebolts to assist in case of a rescue that also offer convenient rappel stations. The East Ledges starts by the trail right below Max's Mayhem and works its way north to Hidden Valley where it is possible to rappel 150 feet off eyebolts to the ground. There are a number of rescues off the East Ledges every year. Tourists are the main culprits as the ledges become exposed and narrow and tend to ice up in cold weather.

NORTH GATEWAY ROCK: WEST FACE

1 **Triple Exposure (12+)** ★★   The hardest route in the Garden, excellent crack climbing with good protection. Gear: To #4 Friend, many Quickdraws. FFA: Richard Aschert, Will Gadd and Dave Dangle, 1986.

2 **Anaconda (11)** ★★★   A Layton Kor aid route and an Earl Wiggins and Jimmy Dunn free climb, what more can you ask for? An all-time Garden classic. Why drive to Moab when you can climb *Anaconda*? Gear: To #4 Friend, Stoppers and RPs. FA: Layton Kor

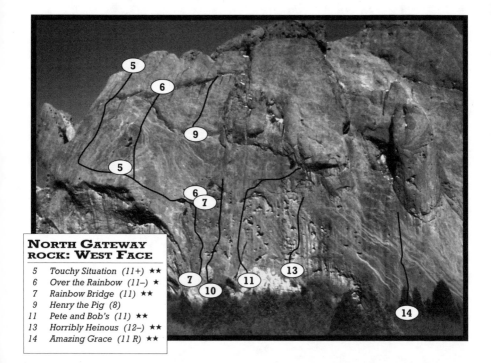

NORTH GATEWAY ROCK: WEST FACE

5	Touchy Situation (11+) ★★
6	Over the Rainbow (11–) ★
7	Rainbow Bridge (11) ★★
9	Henry the Pig (8)
11	Pete and Bob's (11) ★★
13	Horribly Heinous (12–) ★★
14	Amazing Grace (11 R) ★★

and Gary Ziegler. FFA: Earl Wiggins, Jimmy Dunn and John Sherwood, 1975.

3   **The Refugee (11+)** ★★
Hard to find but well worth the effort to get to. Gear: Stoppers, Quickdraws and long slings for potholes. FA: Mark Rolofson and Bob D' Antonio, 1983.

4   **Water Crack (9+)**   Earl Wiggins and John Sherwood, 1975.

5   **Touchy Situation (11+)** ★★
Lots of hard climbing, great position, do it. Gear: Quickdraws. FA: Richard Aschert and Scott Szcyzmak, 1985.

6   **Over the Rainbow (11−)**
★   Good position, somewhat loose rock. Gear: Quickdraws. FA: Ed Webster, Bryan Becker and Leonard Coyne, 1978.

7   **Rainbow Bridge (11)** ★★   Great climbing, a little runout getting to belay. Gear: Quickdraws and #3 Friend. FA: Ed Webster and Peter Mayfield, 1979.

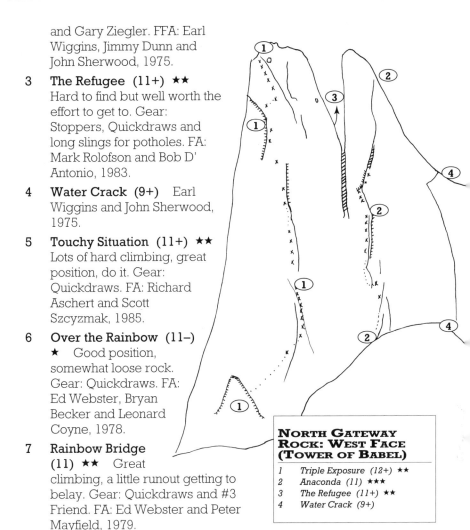

NORTH GATEWAY ROCK: WEST FACE (TOWER OF BABEL)		
1	*Triple Exposure (12+)*	★★
2	*Anaconda (11)*	★★★
3	*The Refugee (11+)*	★★
4	*Water Crack (9+)*	

8   **Borghoff's Blunder (10)** ★   Pretty good route for being a blunder. Gear: #3, #3.5 Friend, Quickdraws. FA: Michael Borghoff, 1960. FFA: Steve Cheyney and Peter Croft, 1960s.

9   **Henry the Pig (8)**   Don't get a ticket climbing this route. Named after the cop who arrested the first ascent party. FA: Leonard Coyne, Ed Bailey and Mark Rolofson, 1976.

10   **Men At Work (11)** ★★★   A Garden classic, the full body lunge should keep you on, or should I say off your toes? FA: Bob D'Antonio and Mark Rolofson, 1983.

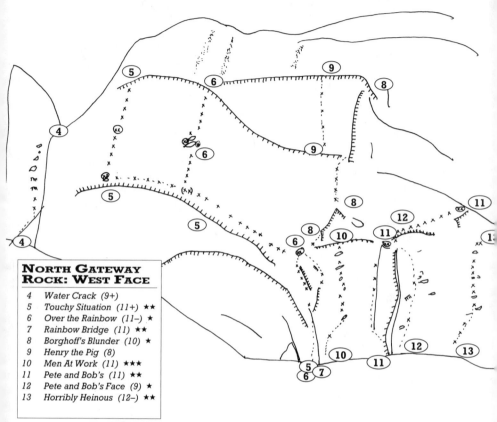

**NORTH GATEWAY
ROCK: WEST FACE**

4   *Water Crack (9+)*
5   *Touchy Situation (11+)* ★★
6   *Over the Rainbow (11–)* ★
7   *Rainbow Bridge (11)* ★★
8   *Borghoff's Blunder (10)* ★
9   *Henry the Pig (8)*
10   *Men At Work (11)* ★★★
11   *Pete and Bob's (11)* ★★
12   *Pete and Bob's Face (9)* ★
13   *Horribly Heinous (12–)* ★★

11   **Pete and Bob's (11)** ★★   The first pitch is one of the most popular in the Garden. FA: Peter Croff and Bob Stauch. FFA: (P1) Steve Cheyney. FFA: Kurt Rasmussen, 1973.

12   **Pete and Bob's Face (9)** ★   FA: Unknown.

13   **Horribly Heinous (12–)** ★★   You don't see a waiting line here! Great moves and hard climbing with some dubious pins for protection. FA: Bob D'Antonio and Mark Rolofson, 1983.

14   **Amazing Grace (11 R)** ★★   An Earl Wiggins classic. Hard moves and long runouts on soft and fragile rock. FA: Earl Wiggins, Leonard Coyne and Ed Webster, 1977.

15   **Saving Grace (9+)**   FA: Ed Webster and Leonard Coyne, 1977.

16   **Escape Gully (9+)**   FA: Harrison Dekker and Sue Patenade, 1982.

17   **Fall from Grace (10 R)** ★   FA: Leonard Coyne, Ed Webster and Ed Russell, 1977.

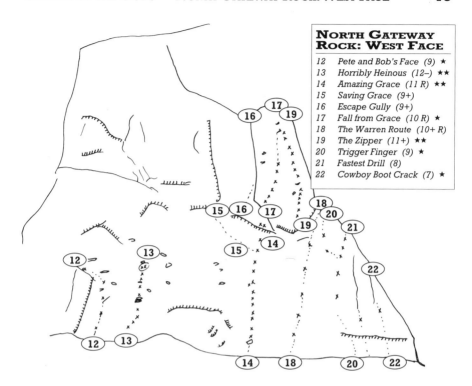

NORTH GATEWAY ROCK: WEST FACE

12	Pete and Bob's Face (9) ★
13	Horribly Heinous (12–) ★★
14	Amazing Grace (11 R) ★★
15	Saving Grace (9+)
16	Escape Gully (9+)
17	Fall from Grace (10 R) ★
18	The Warren Route (10+ R)
19	The Zipper (11+) ★★
20	Trigger Finger (9) ★
21	Fastest Drill (8)
22	Cowboy Boot Crack (7) ★

18 **The Warren Route (10+ R)**   Very long runouts on fairly good rock. FA: Robert Warren and Mike Johnson, 1983.

19 **The Zipper (11+) ★★**   Good moves, excellent position, some bolts may be loose. Gear: #3, #3.5, #4 Friends and Quickdraws. FA: Harvey Carter and Cleve McCarty, 1962. FFA: Mark Rolofson and Jeff Britt, 1984.

20 **Trigger Finger (9) ★**   Good climbing and great protection. FA: Dirk Tyler and Dave Hodges, 1979.

21 **Fastest Drill (8)**   FA: Ed Webster, Mack Johnson and Dave Sweet, 1978.

22 **Cowboy Boot Crack (7) ★**   Very popular. Gear: medium Friends, Stoppers and Quickdraws. FA: Unknown.

NORTH GATEWAY ROCK: WEST FACE (THE FINGER FACE)

This wall provides a number of well-protected high-angle face climbs on holds that vary from solid to very loose. When climbing on loose holds pull down not out! All routes are fixed unless noted.

23 **Bald but Hairy (9+)**   Bad protection on this one. FA: Gary and Mark Hopkin, 1978.

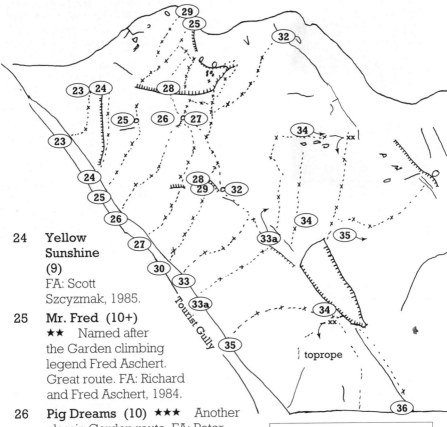

24   Yellow Sunshine (9) FA: Scott Szcyzmak, 1985.

25   Mr. Fred (10+) ★★ Named after the Garden climbing legend Fred Aschert. Great route. FA: Richard and Fred Aschert, 1984.

26   Pig Dreams (10) ★★★ Another classic Garden route. FA: Peter Gallagher and Fred Aschert, 1981.

27   Chatters (9+) ★ FA: Bob Robertson, Bob D'Antonio and Larry Kledzik, 1982.

28   Fatal Curiosity (11 R/X) Be prepared for long runouts with no gear. Gear: #2½ Tri-cam. FA: Richard Aschert, 1985.

29   Dancing in Swineland (10+) ★ Can pigs dance? FA: Pete Williams and Peter Gallagher, 1979.

30   No Ethics Required (10–) Sounds like Shelf Road. FA: Dave Bowmen and Bob Robertson, 1980.

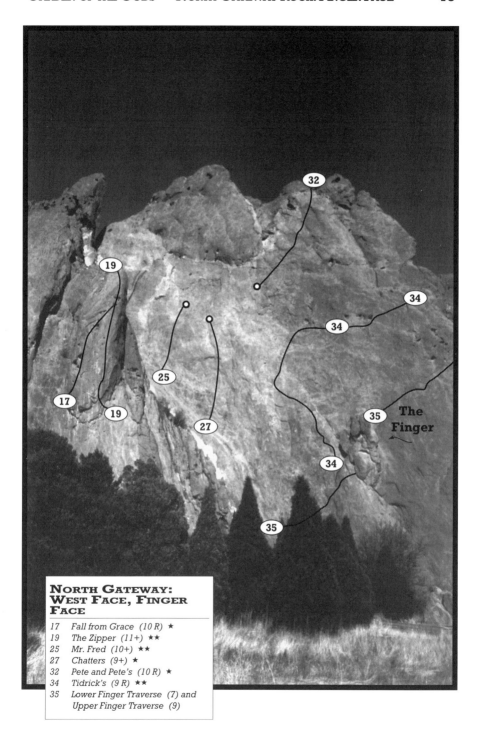

**NORTH GATEWAY:
WEST FACE, FINGER
FACE**

17   Fall from Grace (10 R) ★
19   The Zipper (11+) ★★
25   Mr. Fred (10+) ★★
27   Chatters (9+) ★
32   Pete and Pete's (10 R) ★
34   Tidrick's (9 R) ★★
35   Lower Finger Traverse (7) and
      Upper Finger Traverse (9)

The
Finger

31   **Dust to Dust (10–)** ★★   Classic, do this route! Gear: medium size nuts for potholes on last pitch. FA: Kim Rodgers and Gary Isaacs, 1973.

32   **Pete and Pete's (10 R)** ★   Loose and runout. FA: Pete Williams and Peter Gallagher, 1979.

33   **Son of Tidricks (8)**   FA: Leonard Coyne and Gary Campbell, 1976.

33a   **A Place in the Sun (8)** ★★   One of the most popular climbs in the Garden.

34   **Tidrick's (9 R)** ★★   A must-do route. FA: Rick Tidrick, 1960.

35   **Lower Finger Traverse (7) and Upper Finger Traverse (9)**   The first pitch is a classic, and not your expected 5.7. FA: Paul Radigen, Art Howells, John Auld and Herby Hendricks.

36   **Finger Ramp (7)** ★★
Runout between first and second bolt. Classic! A little thrilling for the second. FA: Richard Borgman and Steve Cheyney, 1960.

37   **Psychic Grandma (9 R)** ★★   This is a girdle traverse of the face, and climbs some nice sections of rock. FA: Pete Croff and Bob Stauch, 1960s.

NORTH GATEWAY ROCK: EAST FACE

38   **Max's Mayhem (10–)** ★   Big hands and some offwidth on somewhat sandy rock. Gear: Large Stoppers, big hexes and Friends. FA: Don Doucette and Max Hinkle, 1965. FFA: (P2) Jim Dunn, Stewart Green and Doug Snively, 1971. FFA: (P1) Kurt Rasmussen and John Hall.

NORTH GATEWAY ROCK: EAST FACE

38   *Max's Mayhem (10-)* ★
39   *Snuggles/Fall Crack (8+)*

39 Snuggles/Fall Crack (8+)   A 5.8 to the
first anchor,(*Snuggles*); 5.8+ to the top
(*Fall Crack*). Gear: Medium Stoppers
and medium to large Friends. FA:
Snuggles, Mike Dudley and
Claudia Pinello, 1960s. *Fall Crack*,
Steve Cheney, 1960s.

40 Spam Man (9)   The first ascent
party used a large pipe in one of
the potholes. FA: Stewart Green
and Leonard Coyne, 1982.

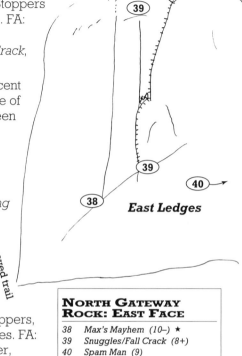

East Ledges

SOUTH GATEWAY ROCK: DRUG WALL

*Drug Wall offers excellent slab climbing
on good rock with reliable
protection. The wall faces
northeast and tends to be
cooler in the summer months
and snowy and cold in the winter
months.*

paved trail

> **NORTH GATEWAY
> ROCK: EAST FACE**
>
> *38   Max's Mayhem (10–)* ★
> *39   Snuggles/Fall Crack (8+)*
> *40   Spam Man (9)*

1 Rhineskeller (8)   Gear: Stoppers,
hexes and runners for potholes. FA:
Bob Stauch and Harvey Carter,
1960s.

2 Candyman (10)   This is a short pitch that starts up in the gully left
of *Cocaine*. FA: Mike Johnson, 1988.

3 The Deal (11+)   Start ten feet right of *Candyman*. FA: Eric
Johnson, 1989.

4 Cocaine (11) ★★★   An all-time Garden classic, great climbing
and excellent rock. FA: Leonard Coyne, Ken Sims and Ed Webster,
1977.

5 Cold Turkey (11+ R) ★★   After the third bolt on *Cocaine*, go left
up the high-angle slab. FA: Bob D'Antonio and Richard Aschert,
1984.

6 Stalagmite (8)   Loose and not worth the effort. Gear: Medium
nuts. FA: Richard Borgman FFA: Dick Long, 1960s?

7 Ninety–Nine Percent Pure (11+) ★★   A good 30-foot variation
to *Cocaine*. FA: Mark Rolofson, 1981.

8 Silver Spoon (6) ★★   An excellent beginner climb. FA: Stewart
Green, Steve Westbay and Kurt Rasmussen, 1971.

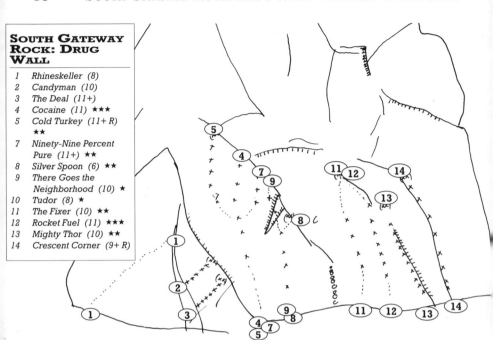

SOUTH GATEWAY ROCK: DRUG WALL

1   Rhineskeller (8)
2   Candyman (10)
3   The Deal (11+)
4   Cocaine (11) ★★★
5   Cold Turkey (11+ R) ★★
7   Ninety-Nine Percent Pure (11+) ★★
8   Silver Spoon (6) ★★
9   There Goes the Neighborhood (10) ★
10 Tudor (8) ★
11 The Fixer (10) ★★
12 Rocket Fuel (11) ★★★
13 Mighty Thor (10) ★★
14 Crescent Corner (9+ R)

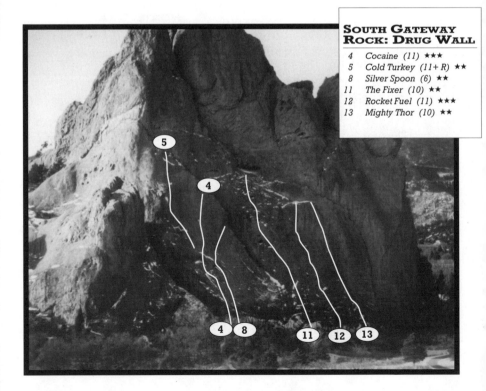

SOUTH GATEWAY ROCK: DRUG WALL

4   Cocaine (11) ★★★
5   Cold Turkey (11+ R) ★★
8   Silver Spoon (6) ★★
11 The Fixer (10) ★★
12 Rocket Fuel (11) ★★★
13 Mighty Thor (10) ★★

9   **There Goes the Neighborhood (10)** ★   Wow! A roof climb climb in the Garden. FA: Peter Gallagher and Brian Becker, 1981.

10   **Tudor (8)** ★   FA: Larry Shubarth and Greg Stevens, 1981.

11   **The Fixer (10)** ★★   Good slab climbing. Rap-off after first pitch as the second is not worth doing. FA: Ed Webster and Leonard Coyne, 1977.

12   **Rocket Fuel (11)** ★★★   One of the best routes in the Garden. FA: Mark Rolofson and Bob D'Antonio, 1983.

13   **Mighty Thor (10)** ★★   Well-protected climbing up the water groove right of *Rocket Fuel.* FA: Mark Rolofson, Bob Robertson, Murray Judge and Gugi Rylegis, 1979.

14   **Crescent Corner (9+ R)**   With better protection this climb would be very popular. FA: Don Peterson and Helmut Husmen, 1971.

SOUTH GATEWAY ROCK: WEST FACE

Good climbs and great western exposure for winter cragging.

15   **Insignificant, But There (10)**   Hard start that leads up to the Practice Slab. FA: Mike Johnson and Bob D'Antonio, 1983.

16   **Practice Slab (1 to 8)** ★   There are a number of ways up the slab, take your pick. Usually toproped. FA: Unknown.

SOUTH GATEWAY ROCK: WEST FACE

16	Practice Slab (1 to 8) ★
17	Tower Crack (10)
19	Kor's Korner (12-) ★★
20	West Point Crack (7+) ★★
22	Indian Head (9+ R)
24	Credibility Gap (9+) ★★★

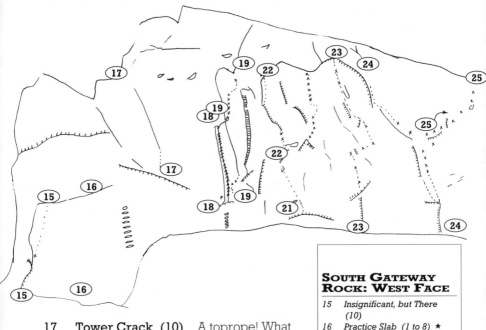

17   **Tower Crack (10)**   A toprope! What more can you say? FA: Bob Robertson, 1982.

18   **Sandman (7)**   If you like dirty and sandy chimney climbing this route is for you. Gear: Large nuts and Friends. FA: Harvey Carter, 1960s.

19   **Kor's Korner (12–)** ★★   A classic route at this grade. Gear: Many Stoppers, Friends to #2 and Quickdraws. FA: Layton Kor and Gary Zielger, 1960s. FFA: Leonard Coyne, 1979.

20   **West Point Crack (7+)** ★★   Very popular, a great outing. Gear: medium to large nuts, slings and Quickdraws. FA: U.S. Army climbers. FFA: Harvey Carter, 1950s.

21   **Pipe Route (10+ R)**   Very serious climbing, this is not a trade route. Gear: Medium nuts, slings, ¼" bolts, hangers and nuts for the second pitch. FA: John Auld and Gary Ziegler. FFA: Earl Wiggins and Jim Souder, 1976.

22   **Indian Head (9+ R)**   Loose climbing up the profile of the Indian Head. Gear: Many Stoppers, nuts and Friends to #3. FA: Steve Hong, Ed Webster and Earl Wiggins, 1976.

23 **Pipe Dreams (10 R) ★★** More like a nightmare. This route is a soft sandstone classic. A must-do for climbers competent at this grade. Gear: Medium to large nuts and Friends. FA: Earl Wiggins, Ed Webster and Steve Hong, 1976.

24 **Credibility Gap (9+) ★★★** This route is a must-do. FA: Gary Zielger and John Auld. FFA: Morgan Gadd and (Leadville 100 winner) Skip Hamilton, 1970.

25 **Dog Day Afternoon (10+)** Long upward traverse. Exposed, wild and rarely done. FA: Mark Rolofson and Ed Webster, 1978.

26 **South End Tower: North Arête (9+)** FA: Harvey Carter, 1982.

27 **South End Tower: South Face (10)** Gear: #6 hex for a pothole and Quickdraws. FA: Harvey Carter, 1982.

28 **Southwest Crack (9)** Gear: Medium nuts, Quickdraws FA: Ed Webster and Harvey Carter, 1982.

MONTEZUMA'S TOWER

This free-standing 120-foot pinnacle has one of the best routes in the Garden on its north ridge.

North Ridge (7+) ★★★ Climb the classic north ridge in two pitches to the top. Rappel west with two ropes to the ground. FA: U.S. Army Climbers, 1940s. FFA: Harvey Carter, 1950.

West Face (8) FA: John Auld.

West Face Direct (11+) Good face climbing up the steep west face of the tower. FA: Jimmy Dunn, (TR) Bob D'Antonio, 1996.

GREY ROCK (AKA KINDERGARDEN ROCK)

This large imposing formation offers some excellent routes with sharp incut edges on compact sandstone. Most of the routes are bolt protected, but it also has some great crack climbing where gear needs to be carried. Park below the southeast buttress on a pullout along the road. There is also excellent bouldering found below the road at the Snake Pit Boulders.

1 **Antline Direct (10 R) ★** Loose climbing on somewhat dubious holds make for a exciting outing. FFA: Bob D'Antonio and Larry Kledzik, 1981.

2 **Skyline Pig (10 R) ★★** Excellent but somewhat runout climbing. Gear: Medium to large Stoppers and slings. FA: Steve Hong and Steve Gropp, 1976.

3 **Question Authority (12) ★★** One of the new sport routes in the Garden. Thin, small edge climbing with two cruxes. FA: Ric Geimen, 1991.

GREY ROCK

1	Antline Direct (10 R) ★
5	Black and Blue (8+ R)
6	Civil Disobedience (12) ★★
9	New Era (7) ★★★
10	End of an Era (8) ★★★

4   **Beat Me Up Scotty (10+)** ★★   Sounds like a personal problem. Excellent climbing on thin flakes and sharp edges. FA: Mike Johnson, 1991.

5   **Black and Blue (8+ R)**   Bad fixed gear and long runouts make this a very unpopular climb. FA: Pete Croff and Steve Cheyney, 1965.

6   **Civil Disobedience (12)** ★★   Thin climbing past the second bolt leads to easier moves and the anchor. FA: Ric Geimen, 1991.

7   **Alligator Soup (11–)** ★   Much safer since the rebolting. Rated 5.11 if you do the second pitch, 5.9+ to the first belay. FA: Leonard Coyne and Ed Russell, 1977.

8   **Diesel and Dust (11–)** ★★   Another excellent recent sport route. Rap the route after the second pitch. FA: Ric and Cindy Giemen, 1990.

9   **New Era (7)** ★★★   This route is pretty hard to miss. Follow the large dihedral for three pitches to the top. Gear: To #3.5 Friend and Quickdraws. FA: Harvey Carter, 1959.

10   **End of an Era (8)** ★★★   Aesthetic face climbing up the arete right of *New Era*. Gear: medium nuts. FA: George Allen and Ann Liebold, 1979.

11   **End to End (10–)** ★★   Excellent overhanging face climbing lead to a rap station. FA: Mike Johnson and Lou Kalina, 1986.

12   **Bob's Buttress Crack (8+)** ★★   More face than crack climbing, excellent. Gear to #3 Friend. FA: Don Doucette and Larry Hazlett, 1967. FFA: Jimmy Dunn and Stewart Green, 1971.

13   **Beginning of the End (9+)** ★★   A little sandy, still a good bolted route. FA: Unknown.

14   **Ormes Chimney (6)**   First done by the great Colorado climbing pioneer Robert Ormes. FA: Robert Ormes, 1925.

GREY ROCK	
1	*Antline Direct (10 R)* ★
2	*Skyline Pig (10 R)* ★★
3	*Question Authority (12)* ★★
4	*Beat Me Up Scotty (10+)* ★★
5	*Black and Blue (8+ R)*
6	*Civil Disobedience (12)* ★★
7	*Alligator Soup (11–)* ★
8	*Diesel and Dust (11–)* ★★
9	*New Era (7)* ★★★
10	*End of an Era (8)* ★★★
11	*End to End (10–)* ★★
12	*Bob's Buttress Crack (8+)* ★★
13	*Beginning of the End (9+)* ★★

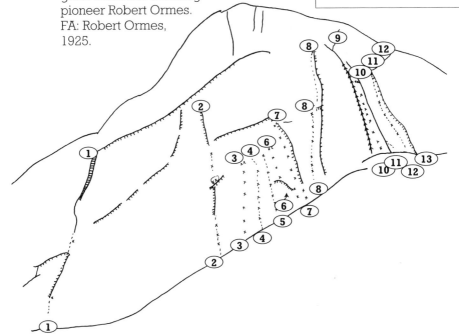

GREY ROCK: WEST FACE

15 **Frankenstein (8 R)** Loose rock and long runouts, this route is not the safest in the Garden. Gear: Long slings for chickenheads. FA: Ken Sims and Leonard Coyne, 1977.

16 **Monster Crack (8)** ★★ Excellent wide crack climbing. Gear: Medium to large Friends. FA: Harvey Carter and Paul Radigen, 1950s.

17 **Scarecrow (10–)** ★★ Thin hand and finger crack climbing. Gear: To #3 Friend. FA: Harvey Carter and Gary Ziegler, 1960s. FFA: Jimmy Dunn and Stewart Green, 1973.

18 **Lance (6)** Not bad for a route done in the 1920s. FA: Albert Ellingwood, 1925.

19 **Footloose and Fancy Free (10)** ★★ A classic route. This is a must—make the effort to do this route. Gear: Medium Stoppers, #2.5, #3 Friends and Quickdraws. FA: Leonard Coyne and Ed Webster, 1977.

20 **Fragile Dihedral (12–)** Flexible holds and hard moves. FA: Bob D'Antonio, 1985.

21 **South End Slabs (2 to 8)** Set up a toprope and have some fun. FA: Unknown.

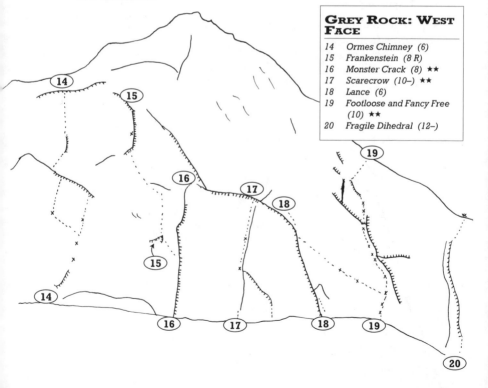

GREY ROCK: WEST FACE

16　Monster Crack (8) ★★
17　Scarecrow (10-) ★★
19　Footloose and Fancy Free
　　(10) ★★

KEYHOLE ROCK

This excellent formation offers a number of great short routes. With eastern and western exposure you can play hide and seek with the sun depending on the season. The rock is broken by many ledges and has easy access on and off the climbs.

EAST FACE
FIRST TIER, SOUTH END

1　**Dancin Fool (9) ★★**　Good climbing on excellent rock. FA: Peter Gallagher and Larry Shubarth, 1980.

2　**True Grit (8 R) ★**　Runouts in some places, this is still a route worth doing. FA: Pete Croff, Leonard Coyne and Mark Rolofson, 1976.

3　**Brand-X Caper (10+ R)**　A long runout getting to the crux keeps most climbers on the ground. FA: Ed Webster, Leonard Coyne, Steve Johnson and Mark Rolofson, 1977.

4　**Buttress Climb (7)**　FA: Harvey Carter, 1975.

SECOND TIER, SOUTH END

5　**South Ridge (7 X)**　Just toprope it. FA: Unknown.

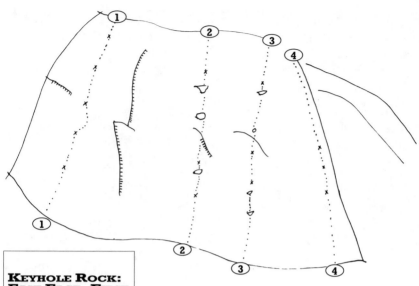

KEYHOLE ROCK: EAST FACE, FIRST TIER, SOUTH END

1 Dancin Fool *(9)* ★★
2 True Grit *(8 R)* ★
3 Brand-X Caper *(10+ R)*
4 Buttress Climb *(7)*

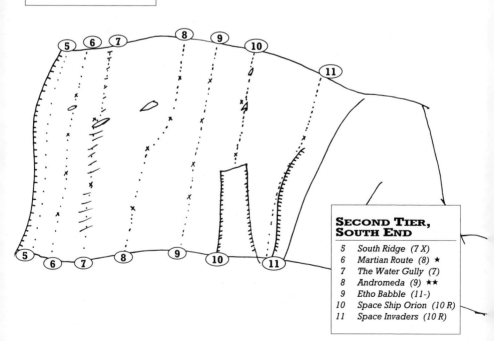

SECOND TIER, SOUTH END

5 South Ridge *(7 X)*
6 Martian Route *(8)* ★
7 The Water Gully *(7)*
8 Andromeda *(9)* ★★
9 Etho Babble *(11-)*
10 Space Ship Orion *(10 R)*
11 Space Invaders *(10 R)*

6   **Martian Route (8) ★**   FA: Unknown Martian, 1981.

7   **The Water Gully (7)**   FA: Unknown.

8   **Andromeda (9) ★★**   FA: Dennis Harmon, Bob D'Antonio and Larry Kledzik, 1982.

9   **Etho Babble (11−)**   FA: Mark Milligan and Brent Kertzman, 1986.

10 **Space Ship Orion (10 R)**   FA: Bob D'Antonio, Dennis Harmon and Larry Kledzik, 1982.

11 **Space Invaders (10 R)**   FA: Bob D'Antonio, Dennis Harmon and Larry Kledzik, 1982.

THIRD TIER, SOUTH END

12 **Macbeth (10) ★★**   A Larry Kledzik classic! FA: Larry Kledzik, 1981.

13 **Cheap Thrills (10)**   FA: Bob D'Antonio and Larry Kledzik, 1982.

14 **Upper Borderline (11)**   FA: Ed Webster and Bob D'Antonio, 1982.

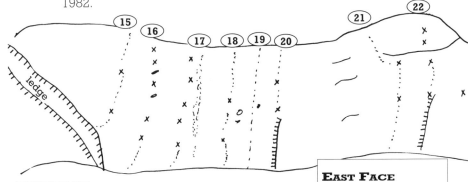

EAST FACE
FIRST TIER, NORTH END

15 **Left Out (11)**   FA: Bob D'Antonio and Gene Smith, 1986.

16 **Shock It to the Top (12) ★★**   Sequential climbing leads to a hard crux move. FA: Gene Smith and Bob D'Antonio, 1986.

17 **Waterchute Route (12−) ★★**   Crux is getting past the first pin. FFA: Bob D'Antonio, 1981.

18 **Patty the Pig (10+) ★★**   Good climbing, be careful getting to the second bolt. FA: Bob D'Antonio and Ed Webster, 1982.

19 **Pig Dust (11+)**   Toprope the route ten feet right of Patty the Pig. FA: Bob D'Antonio and Mark Rolofson, 1983.

EAST FACE FIRST TIER, NORTH END

15 *Left Out (11)*
16 *Shock It to the Top (12)* ★★
17 *Waterchute Route (12−)* ★★
18 *Patty the Pig (10+)* ★★
19 *Pig Dust (11+)*
20 *Rocket Dust (10)* ★
21 *Prodigal Son (9−)*
22 *The Morning After (10+)* ★★

20   **Rocket Dust** (10) ★   FA: Bob D'Antonio (solo), 1983.

21   **Prodigal Son** (9–)   FA: Peter Gallagher and Larry Shubarth, 1981.

22   **The Morning After** (10+) ★★   Mark Rolofson and Bob Robertson, 1980.

SECOND TIER, NORTH END

23   **Hound Dog** (7)   Gear: Medium nuts and Friends. FA: Harvey Carter?

24   **Finger Banger** (10) ★   Gear: medium Stoppers and Quickdraws. FA: Bob D'Antonio, 1982.

25   **Status Quo** (9)   FA: Bob D'Antonio and Harvey Carter, 1982.

26   **Welcome to the Garden** (10) ★   FA: Bob D'Antonio and Ed Webster, 1982.

WEST FACE

27   **Borderline** (10) ★★   Gear: #2 and #2.5 Friends and Quickdraws. FA: Harvey Carter. FFA: Earl Wiggins, Leonard Coyne and Mark Rolofson, 1977.

28   **Small Overhang** (10)   FA: (TR) Bob Robertson and Fred Aschert, 1981.

29   **BFD** (10) ★★   FA: Bob D'Antonio and Peter Gallagher, 1981.

SECOND TIER, NORTH END
23   *Hound Dog (7)*
24   *Finger Banger (10)* ★
25   *Status Quo (9)*
26   *Welcome to the Garden (10)* ★

ledge

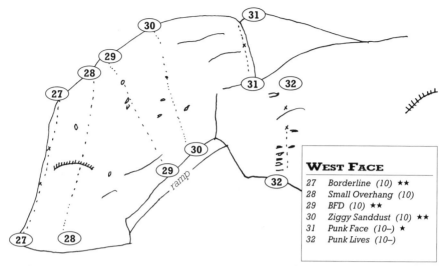

WEST FACE

27 Borderline (10) ★★
28 Small Overhang (10)
29 BFD (10) ★★
30 Ziggy Sanddust (10) ★★
31 Punk Face (10–) ★
32 Punk Lives (10–)

30 **Ziggy Sanddust (10) ★★** FA: Bob D'Antonio, Peter Gallagher and Larry Kledzik, 1981.

31 **Punk Face (10–) ★** FA: Bob D'Antonio and Larry Kledzik, 1981.

32 **Punk Lives (10–)** FA: Bob D'Antonio and Larry Kledzik, 1981.

33 **Old Aid Bolts (10+ R)** Three hundred feet down and right of *Punk Lives* you'll see a couple old bolts on a short face. FA: Bob D'Antonio, 1982.

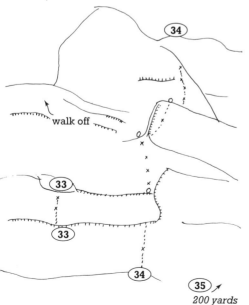

34 **Mission Impossible (11 R)** ★★ This route ascends the west face of Keyhole in four short pitches. FA: Harvey Carter. FFA: Bob D'Antonio, 1982.

35 **Tempest (10+)** About 200 feet right of *Mission Impossible* are two thin-looking crack lines, Tempest is the right one. Gear: Medium wired Stoppers, #4 Friend and slings for potholes. FA: Ed Webster and Mike Johnson, 1982.

WEST FACE

34 Mission Impossible (11 R) ★★
35 Tempest (10+)

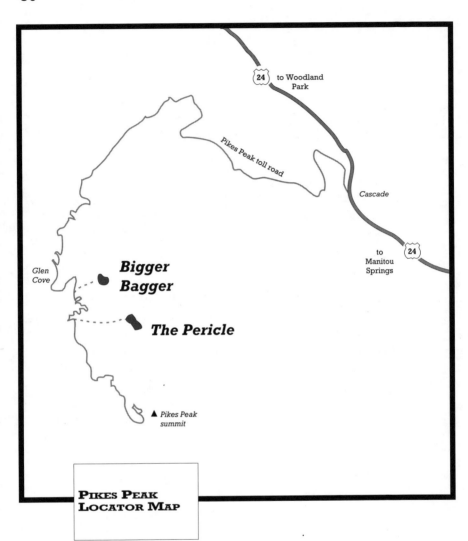

Glen
Cove

**Bigger
Bagger**

The Pericle

▲ Pikes Peak
summit

24 to Woodland
Park

Pikes Peak toll road

Cascade

to
Manitou
Springs

24

**PIKES PEAK
LOCATOR MAP**

SECTION TWO

PIKES PEAK

For great crack climbing in a beautiful alpine setting, Bigger Bagger and The Pericle Cliffs located on the eastern flank of the Pikes Peak massif have some of the most splendid and accessible alpine climbing in the United States.

The cracks are long and continuous on superb pink and white granite, unusually solid for alpine rock. The cliffs offer three- to four-pitch climbs (500- to 600-foot) moderate approaches and great natural protection.

Most of the climbing is located at 12,000 ft. above sea level. The climbing season is short, May to September in most years. Be aware of objective dangers. Be prepared for problems that are associated with climbs in the mountains.

These are not sport climbs! You must be able to climb or retreat in the face of less than ideal conditions. Bring extra clothing and gear. The pitches are long and at this altitude very strenuous! Be self-reliant, know your limits. This is a place where high numbers and bolt clipping takes a back seat to adventure and the outdoor experience.

HOW TO GET THERE   Take I-25 to US Highway 24 west to the Cascade exit. Follow the signs to the Pikes Peak Toll Road. For Bigger Bagger go 15.2 miles up the toll road. Park at the second major switchback. Then hike two moderate miles southeast to the base of the cliff. For Pericle Rock, park at 16.7 miles on the road. Then hike along the crest of the ridge down into the Bottomless Pit to the cliffs. The road to the cliffs is a toll road. There is no camping along the road and the gate to the road is locked after 10 p.m. There could be problems if you don't make the cutoff time. Please ask what time the gate is locked when paying your toll.

PERICLE ROCK

1   **Voodoo Arch** (10+)   For this route follow the obvious left-slanting arch just left of *Free and Easy*. Classic. Gear: To #3.5 Friends. FA: Harvey Miller and Brian Teale.

2   **Free and Easy (II 7)**   Follow the obvious chimney on the far left
     side of the crag. Rated 5.8 if you take the obvious handcrack on the
     last pitch. Gear: To #4 Friends. FA: Harvey Carter and Art Howells,
     1960s.

3   **Don't Think Twice (III 9)** ★★   Great three-pitch handcrack 30
     feet right of *Free and Easy*. Gear: To #3.5 Friends. FA: Billy
     Westbay and Cito Kirkpatrick, 1973.

4   **Arching Jams (III 10)** ★★★   One of the best crack climbs in
     Colorado. Follow the obvious double arches for three pitches to
     top. Gear: To #3.5 Friends. FA: Mark Hesse and Dan McClure.
     FFA: Dan McClure and Billy Westbay, 1972.

5   **Pericle Chimney (III 11-)** ★   Offwidth climbing at 12,000 feet.
     Boy, what a treat. Follow the left-leaning crack just right of *Arching*

Jams. Pitch 3 is the same as *Arching Jams*. Gear: To #4 Friends or larger. FA: Dan McClure, Billy Westbay and Mark Hesse, 1972. FFA: Earl Wiggins and Jon Sherwood.

6   **Feather Route (III 11–)**   Start just right of Pericle Chimney. Strenuous crack climbing for three pitches. Gear: To #3.5 Friends. FA: Dan McClure and Mark Hesse FFA: Dan McClure and Earl Wiggins, 1974.

7   **Around the Corner (II 10)**   Loose third pitch. Can rappel from the end of the second pitch. Gear: To #3 Friends. FA: Billy Westbay and Cito Kirkpatrick, 1973.

8   **Mean and Nasty (10+)** ★   Jimmy Dunn decribed this route as a hard two-pitch flaring crack climb right of *Around the Corner*. Gear: Many medium Friends, Stoppers and small camming devices. FA: Jimmy Dunn, 1975.

9   **Stemulation (II 12–)** ★★   Hard stemming up a beautiful corner. This route is located on the south-facing wall when walking to the base of the cliff. Gear: Rack to #2.5 Friends. FA: Glenn Schuler and Rickey Westbay, 1994.

Pericle Rock
1   Voodoo Arch (10+)
2   Free and Easy (II 7)
3   Don't Think Twice (III 9)
4   Arching Jams (III 10) ★★★
5   Pericle Chimney (III 11–)
6   Feather Route (III 11–)
7   Around the Corner (II 10)
8   Mean and Nasty (10+) ★
9   Stemulation (II 12–) ★★

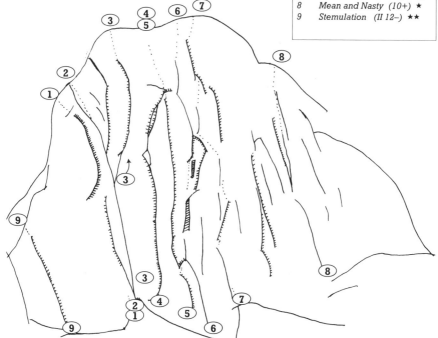

BIGGER BAGGER

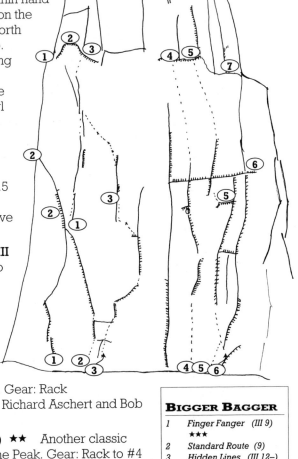

1   **Finger Fanger   (III 9)**
★★★   Excellent thin hand and finger crack on the first pitch. Well worth the effort to get to. Gets early morning sun. Gear: To #3 Friends. FA: Steve Cheyney and Earl Wiggins, 1971.

2   **Standard Route**
(9)   The route tends to wander. Gear: Rack to #3.5 Friend. FA: Don Doucette and Steve Cheyney.

3   **Hidden Lines   (III 12–)** ★★   Not so hidden once you start climbing. Same start as *Standard Route*. Go right after 50 feet up shallow cracks. Some fixed gear. Gear: Rack to #3 Friend. FA: Richard Aschert and Bob Robertson, 1987.

4   **Gold Wall (10–)** ★★   Another classic crack climb on the Peak. Gear: Rack to #4 Friend FA: Don Doucette.

5   **Walk on the Wild Side (10)** ★★   A Lou Reed classic, also a pretty good climb. Gear: rack to #4 Friend. FA: Kevin Murray and Mark Rolofson, 1978.

6   **Solar Winds (11)** ★   If hard offwidth climbing at 11,000 feet is your bag, this climb is for you. Gear: Rack to #4 Friend. FA: Leonard Coyne and Mark Rolofson, 1978.

7   **Neutron Tide (11+)**   Basically a one-pitch variation. Gear: Rack to #2.5 Friend. FA: Leonard Coyne and Peter Mayfield.

BIGGER BAGGER
1   *Finger Fanger   (III 9)* ★★★
2   *Standard Route   (9)*
3   *Hidden Lines   (III 12–)* ★★
4   *Gold Wall   (10–)* ★★
5   *Walk on the Wild Side (10)* ★★
6   *Solar Winds   (11)* ★
7   *Neutron Tide   (11+)*

SILVER CASCADE SLAB (AKA HESITATION SLAB)

This excellent piece of granite located in Upper North Cheyenne Canyon offers some of the most convenient and enjoyable slab climbing in the Pikes Peak Area. The rock is compact and solid, unlike the rock in the lower canyon. The protection is good and the descent off the rock is easy, making for an enjoyable outing.

The slab is reached by walking up a short, steep trail from the Helen Hunt Falls parking area. The left side of the slab is less angled and has a number of moderate routes that end on the summit. The right side of the slab is accessed by scrambling up the wide sloping ramp that cuts the rock in half. Please watch out for loose rock and dropping any loose debris down the descent trail as this is a popular tourist attraction.

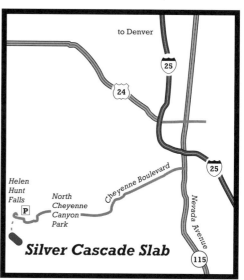

HOW TO GET THERE   *From Colorado Springs exit I-25 at South Nevada Ave. Head southwest down Nevada to Cheyenne Boulevard. Go right at the canyon entrance. Head up North Cheyenne Canyon to Helen Hunt Falls parking area. Follow a trail up past the falls to the base of the cliff.*

1   **Silver Left (6)**   First route on the far left side of the slab. FA: Harvey Carter.

2   **Tunnel Vision (7)**   A great route with fun moves and good protection. FA: Unknown.

3   **Ladder Route (6)**   This is the first bolted route on the left side of the slab. FA: Stewart and Nancy Green, 1993.

4   **Robertson Wall (7)**   Watch out for old bolts and long runouts. FA: Bob Robertson.

5   **Chronic Bedwetter (7)**   Good protection and moderate climbing make for a great outing. Be sure to change the sheets. FA: Stewart and Brett Spencer-Green, 1993.

6   **Reality Check (8)**   Edge and smear your way pass seven bolts to the summit. High quality. FA: Stewart Green, Erick Christianson, Mark Van Horn and Chuck Carlson, 1993.

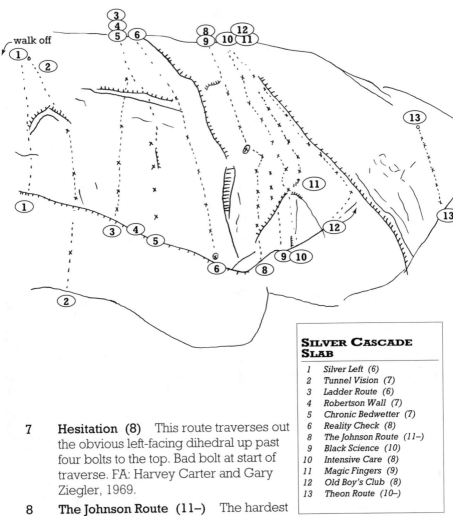

SILVER CASCADE SLAB

1	Silver Left (6)
2	Tunnel Vision (7)
3	Ladder Route (6)
4	Robertson Wall (7)
5	Chronic Bedwetter (7)
6	Reality Check (8)
8	The Johnson Route (11–)
9	Black Science (10)
10	Intensive Care (8)
11	Magic Fingers (9)
12	Old Boy's Club (8)
13	Theon Route (10–)

7   Hesitation (8)   This route traverses out the obvious left-facing dihedral up past four bolts to the top. Bad bolt at start of traverse. FA: Harvey Carter and Gary Ziegler, 1969.

8   The Johnson Route (11–)   The hardest route on the crag also offers good climbing and protection. FA: Mike Johnson.

9   Black Science (10)   Take a line over the obvious roof. A medium Friend protects the moves over the roof. FA: Stewart and Ian Spencer-Green, 1993.

10   Intensive Care (8)   Hopefully you won't be in intensive when you finish this route. Bring a large Friend for the first moves. You'll need a 165-foot rope to do this pitch in one lead. FA: Stewart Green and Ian Spencer-Green, 1993.

11   **Magic Fingers** (9)   Start the same as *Intensive Care*. Go up and right after the roof up the slab past the bolts to the top. Hangers are currently missing. FA: Stewart Green, Dennis Jackson and Yvonne Bolton, 1993.

12   **Old Boy's Club** (8)   Scramble across the sloping ledge to a belay with pitons. Follow a line of bolts to the left of the rotten chimney. FA: Stewart Green and Dennis Jackson, 1993.

13   **Theon Route** (10–)   On far right side of cliff, past six bolts. FA: Jim Theon, 1995.

EMILY DANTI ON *CHATTERS* (5.9+) GARDEN OF THE GODS. PHOTO BY STEWART M. GREEN.

MARTHA MORRIS ON *CRACK OF CONSCIOUSNESS* (5.9), TABLE MOUNTAIN. PHOTO BY STEWART M. GREEN

SECTION THREE

TABLE MOUNTAIN
COLORADO SPRINGS

This new sport climbing crag, located just south of Colorado Springs, offers a number of quality short sport routes with excellent protection on high quality sandstone. The routes range in height from 30 to 65 feet. The cliffs are surrounded by juniper, piñon and ponderosa pines with beautiful vistas of the Sangre de Cristo range to the west. Shambhala is the main climbing area and has 25 well-bolted sport routes. Aryuveda is a bouldering area located 1.8 miles down the road to the west. This area is designated State Game lands and has only recently been opened for public use. Please be aware of other land users (hunters and hikers) and treat them with the same respect that you would expect. Camping is allowed from September through December in designated areas. Please do not litter, dispose of human waste properly.

HOW TO GET THERE   From Colorado Springs, go south on Colorado 115 (Nevada Avenue). At

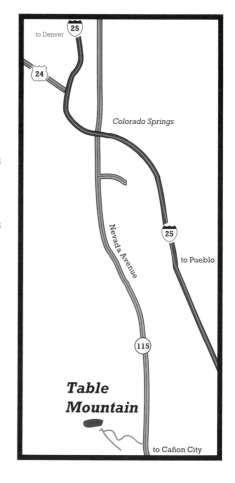

the main gate of Fort Carson Army Base, the four-lane highway turns into
two lanes, set your odometer here. Continue for 15.5 miles to a turnoff on
the right marked "Table Mountain." From this point you will be able to see
the cliffs. To reach the main cliff (Shambhala) go 1.9 miles to a pullout along
the road, then follow a faint trail through a meadow and into a talus field
below the right side of the cliff. Stay on the right side of the talus to the cliff
base. All you need to climb here is eight to ten Quickdraws and a 165-foot
rope. All the routes were put up by Mark Van Horn, Erick Christiansen and
Ed Schmidt. To reach the bouldering (Aryuveda), continue on the road for
another 1.8 miles to a pulloff by an old quarry.

   1   Suicide Drive (9+) ★
   2   Material Tissue (10+) ★★
   3   Clear Your Head (10–) ★
   4   Black Frye (12–) ★★
   5   Free Radicals (12–) ★★★
   6   Snow Babies (12–) ★★★
   7   The Buddha Wears Climbing Shoes (10) ★
   8   Spring Loose (10+) ★
   9   Rock Shox (11) ★
  10   I Ain't Blind (9) ★★
  11   Call It What You Want (10) ★★

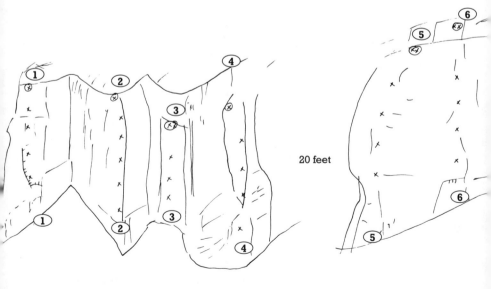

20 feet

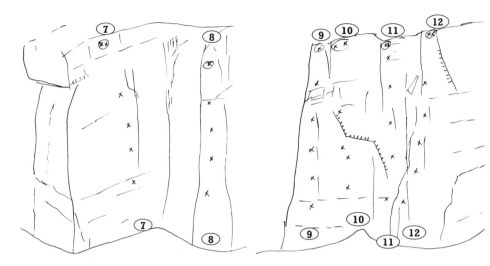

12   Sweet Thang (10) ★★★
13   Middle of Doubt (10)
14   Sole Rite (10) ★
15   Magical Blend (11+) ★★
16   Movers and Shakers (9+)

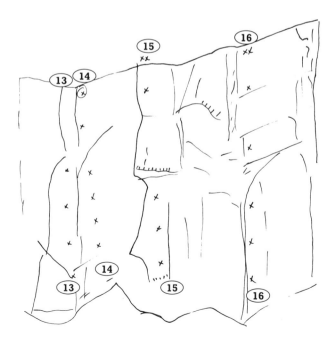

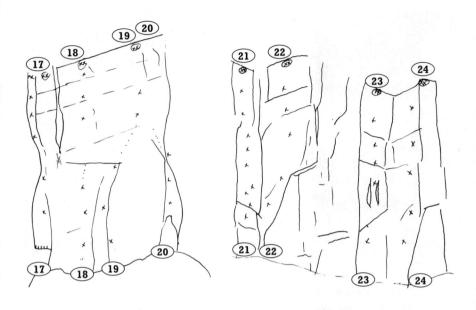

17   Twisted Travels (11) ★★★
18   If It's Free, It's for Me (10−) ★★
19   Question Reality (11+) ★
20   Toxic Faith (9)
21   Positions Available (12−) ★
22   Gonzaga (10+) ★
23   Freak'n on Friction (9+) ★
24   Crack of Consciousness (9)

BOB D'ANTONIO ON
TWISTED TRAVELS (5.11),
TABLE MOUNTAIN. PHOTO
BY STEWART M. GREEN

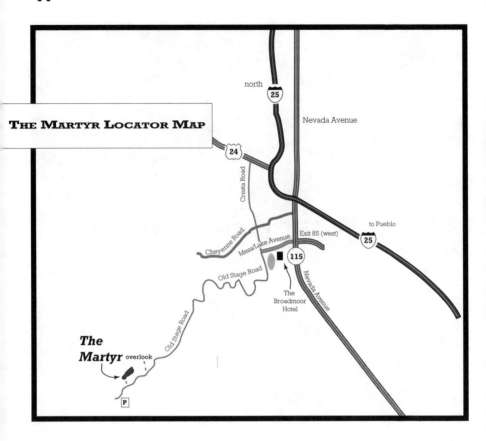

THE MARTYR LOCATOR MAP

north

25

Nevada Avenue

24

Cresta Road

to Pueblo

Cheyenne Road

Mesa/Lake Avenue

Exit 85 (west)

25

115

Nevada Avenue

Old Stage Road

The
Broadmoor
Hotel

**The
Martyr** overlook

Old Stage Road

P

SECTION FOUR

AIGUILLE DE ST. PETER and THE MARTYR

This hard-to-find area offers a handful of traditional routes in a remote setting on the south side of Pikes Peak. The crags are located on a ridge high above the old Gold Camp mining road. This road connects the old mining town of Cripple Creek to Colorado Springs. Being only 20 miles away from a major city gives the area a feeling of being remote. This is a great place to climb; it offers a semi-alpine setting, classic routes and very few people.

In the early 1960s, Steve Cheyney, Peter Croff and Bob Stauch added two very impressive climbs, *The Martyr* (5.9+) and *Pearly Gates* (5.10–). Though not too hard by today's standards, they were very cutting edge in the early '60s. *The Martyr* is still the best route in the area and offers 300 feet of great crack climbing. *Pearly Gates* is not to be missed, giving great thin crack climbing up the center of a beautiful 200-foot, high-angle slab.

HOW TO GET THERE   Take the Nevada Street exit off I-25. Turn west onto Cheyenne Road to Cresta; turn left onto Cresta. Make a right onto Mesa, then to the back of The Broadmoor where it will intersect with Old Stage Road. Turn right. From the beginning of Old Stage Road, go 18 miles up the road to the St. Peter's overlook. Park at a two- to three-car pullout located 0.25 mile past the overlook. Lock your car, then walk 0.5 mile up the steep slope to the north.

THE MARTYR
1   **The Martyr (9+) ★★★**   Follow the obvious finger-and-hand crack on the left side of the rock. This route alone is worth the effort. Gear: Rack to #3.5 Friends. FA: Steve Cheyney, Pete Croff and Bob Stuach, 1964.

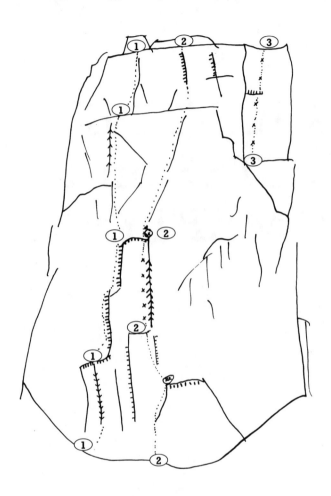

THE MARTYR

1	The Martyr (9+)	★★★
2	The Athenian Arête (12–)	★
3	The Oracle (11+)	★★

2   **The Athenian Arête (12–)** ★   The arête 25 feet right of *The Martyr*. It is best to climb up 40 feet to a ledge and belay at some bolts at the start of the arête. Look hard for the bolts. Gear: To #3 Friend. FA: Mark Van Horn and Erick Christianson, 1993.

3   **The Oracle (11+) ★★**   This is a great one-pitch route up the west face of the summit block. Gear: Six Quickdraws and a #2.5 Friend. FA: Mark Van Horn, 1993.

THE PEARLY GATES

4   **Pearly Gates (10–) ★★★**   This is a classic route, climb the thin fingercrack up the slab. Gear: To #2 Friends, RPs. FA: Steve Cheyney, Pete Croff and Bob Stauch, 1964.

5   **The Ascension (9) ★**   The route is ten feet right of *Pearly Gates*. Good slab climbing on great rock. Gear: To #1.5 Friend, include eight Quickdraws. FA: Mark Van Horn, 1993.

6   **Devotion (11+) ★★**   This route is best approached by rappel. As you come through the notch on the approach to *The Martyr*, instead of going right to *The Martyr*, go straight to a tree, then look over the edge for bolts and rappel from the tree. Gear: Nine Quickdraws and small camming gear. FA: Mark Van Horn 1993.

THE SANCTUM

All the cracks in The Sanctum, the cliff above The Pearly Gates, were climbed in the 1970s by Billy Westbay, Stewart Green, Dan Mc Clure and Doug Snively. In keeping with area tradition, the routes are not named or rated.

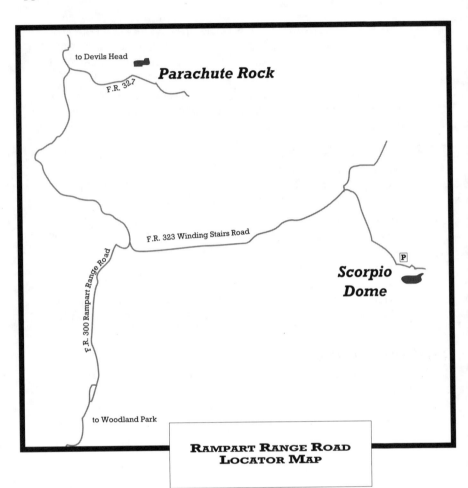

to Devils Head

Parachute Rock

F.R. 32.7

F.R. 323 Winding Stairs Road

F.R. 300 Rampart Range Road

P

Scorpio Dome

to Woodland Park

RAMPART RANGE ROAD LOCATOR MAP

SECTION FIVE

RAMPART RANGE ROAD

Rampart Range Road slices its way to Denver from its origin at the Garden of the Gods in Colorado Springs. High above the town of Woodland Park, the road allows access to a number of Pike National Forest service roads. Along these roads lie a number of interesting granite crags. Though the area has barely been tapped for climbing potential, a few of the more accessible crags have seen some activity and have produced a number of excellent routes in a semi-remote setting.

The south-facing crags offer excellent cragging in spring and fall. Snow or wet weather can present a problem with access. When the roads are wet or snowy they should only be attempted with a four-wheel drive vehicle. The camping is primitive so feel free to camp at any spots along the service roads. The potential in this area is mind-boggling. There are literally hundreds of small crags waiting to be explored. Any new route information should be sent to Chockstone Press.

HOW TO GET THERE   From I-25 in Colorado Springs, take US 24 west to Woodland Park, turn right at the McDonald's on Baldwin Avenue which will turn into Rampart Range Road. Set your odometer here. Follow Rampart Range Road and bear left at all turns. At 4.2 miles, the road turns to gravel and you will see signs for FR 300 (Rampart Range Road). Continue to 10.3 miles; to get to Scorpio Dome turn right on FR 323, go 3.5 miles to a pullout parking area on the right. Walk down the road to the saddle behind Scorpio Dome, turn west at the rock and follow a short trail down a gully to the west side of the summit block. Drop down then crawl under the block's edge to a ledge. The Scorpio Crack is very obvious and should be right above you.

DOCTOR DREAM

From FR 300, turn right onto FR 322 and follow to an obvious cluster of rocks in a beautiful meadow with beaver ponds.

> **Doctor Dream (12+)** ★★   The obvious overhanging crack splitting the northwest face. Gear: Small camming gear, Friends to #2. FA: Bob D'Antonio, 1985.

SCORPIO DOME

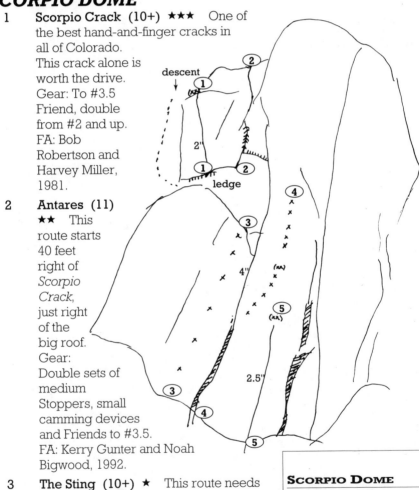

1   **Scorpio Crack (10+)** ★★★   One of the best hand-and-finger cracks in all of Colorado. This crack alone is worth the drive. Gear: To #3.5 Friend, double from #2 and up. FA: Bob Robertson and Harvey Miller, 1981.

2   **Antares (11)** ★★   This route starts 40 feet right of *Scorpio Crack,* just right of the big roof. Gear: Double sets of medium Stoppers, small camming devices and Friends to #3.5. FA: Kerry Gunter and Noah Bigwood, 1992.

3   **The Sting (10+)** ★   This route needs some new bolts! Starts on the slab below *Scoprio Crack.* Gear: Quickdraws. FA: Bob Robertson, 1985.

SCORPIO DOME	
1	*Scorpio Crack (10+)* ★★★
2	*Antares (11)* ★★
3	*The Sting (10+)* ★
4	*Harvey's Crack (9)*
5	*Andromeda Strain (11+)*

4   **Harvey's Crack (9)**   Start in the obvious chimney crack just right of *The Sting*. Gear: To #4 Friends. FA: Harvey Carter, 1982?

5   **Andromeda Strain (11+)**   Go 40 feet up *Harvey's Crack*. Step right to a dish and follow the line of bolts. Gear: Friends for crack, Quickdraws. FA: Kerry Gunter and Bob Couchman, 1990.

6   **Orion (10-)** ★   Starts 50 feet down and right of *Andromeda Strain*. Gear: To #3.5 Friends. FA: Kerry Gunter and Noah Bigwood, 1990.

PARACHUTE ROCK

This excellent crag has a handful of one-pitch climbs on solid granite. It is a great area for climbers to learn how to place natural gear as the wall offers excellent crack climbing with good protection. The views from the top of the rock are worth the trip.

Where the road turns to dirt, set your odometer and go 12.5 miles on FR 300 (Rampart Range Road) to FR 327. Turn right 0.75 mile to a pulloff. Hike 0.5 mile up to the crag.

1   **Miss Bliss (7)** ★★   Excellent face climbing past two bolts on the far left side of the rock. Gear: Small cams and Quickdraws. FA: Stewart Green and Martha Morris, 1996.

2   **Burgers (9-)** ★   Follows a thin crack to a lone bolt. Gear: Small Stoppers, cams and Quickdraws. FA: Tom Austin, 1980.

3   **Texas D.J. (10-)** ★   Starts five feet right of *Burgers*. Gear: Small cams, Stoppers and Quickdraws. FA: Bob D'Antonio and Dennis Jackson, 1996.

4   **Unknown (6)** ★   Great route for climbers just learning how to place natural gear. Gear: Small to medium Stoppers and Friends. FA: Tom Austin and Steve Cheney, 1980?

5   **Unknown (5)** ★   Another good route for novice climbers. Gear: Small to medium Stoppers and Friends. FA: The Cobbler Crew, 1980.

6   **Unknown (9)** ★   Good thin face and crack climbing up a steep wall to a large ledge. Gear: Small Stoppers, RPs and Friends. FA: The Cobbler Crew, 1980.

7   **The Caped One (9+)** ★★   Excellent thin hand-and-finger crack. Gear: Small to medium Stoppers and Friends. FA: The Cobbler Crew, 1980.

8   **The Grunt (9)**   Obvious right-facing offwidth corner. Gear: Medium to large Friends. FA: The Cobbler Crew, 1980.

9　**True Religion (10+)** ★★　This route follows the obvious overhanging right-facing corner on the west face of the rock. Gear: Stoppers and small camming gear. FA: Mack Johnson, 1980.

10　**Rip Cord (10)** ★★　Great thin hand jamming up a steep wall. Gear: Medium to large Friends. FA: The Cobbler Crew, 1980.

11　**Lost Cord (11)** ★★　Awesome handcrack on the backside of the rock (north face). Gear: Medium Friends. FA: Bob D'Antonio, Peter Gallagher and Bob Robertson, 1981.

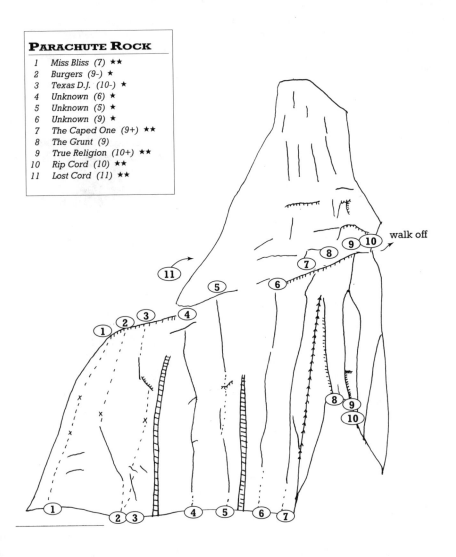

PARACHUTE ROCK

1	*Miss Bliss (7)* ★★
2	*Burgers (9-)* ★
3	*Texas D.J. (10-)* ★
4	*Unknown (6)* ★
5	*Unknown (5)* ★
6	*Unknown (9)* ★
7	*The Caped One (9+)* ★★
8	*The Grunt (9)*
9	*True Religion (10+)* ★★
10	*Rip Cord (10)* ★★
11	*Lost Cord (11)* ★★

walk off

INDEX

Bolded numbers refer to topos or photos of the feature or route. Formations and areas are in all captials.

Access: It's everybody's concern

the **ACCESS FUND**

The **Access Fund,** a national, non-profit climbers' organization, is working to keep you climbing. The Access Fund helps preserve access and protect the environment by providing funds for land acquisitions and climber support facilities, financing scientific studies, publishing educational materials promoting low-impact climbing, and providing start-up money, legal counsel and other resources to local climbers' coalitions.

Climbers can help preserve access by being responsible users of climbing areas. Here are some practical ways to support climbing:

- **COMMIT YOURSELF TO "LEAVING NO TRACE."** Pick up litter around campgrounds and the crags. Let your actions inspire others.

- **DISPOSE OF HUMAN WASTE PROPERLY.** Use toilets whenever possible. If none are available, choose a spot at least 50 meters from any water source. Dig a hole 6 inches (15 cm) deep, and bury your waste in it. *Always pack out toilet paper* in a Ziploc™-type bag.

- **UTILIZE EXISTING TRAILS.** Avoid cutting switchbacks and trampling vegetation.

- **USE DISCRETION WHEN PLACING BOLTS AND OTHER "FIXED" PROTECTION.** Camouflage all anchors with rock-colored paint. Use chains for rappel stations, or leave rock-colored webbing.

- **RESPECT RESTRICTIONS THAT PROTECT NATURAL RESOURCES AND CULTURAL ARTIFACTS.** Appropriate restrictions can include prohibition of climbing around Indian rock art, pioneer inscriptions, and on certain formations during raptor nesting season. Power drills are illegal in wilderness areas. *Never chisel or sculpt holds in rock on public lands, unless it is expressly allowed* – no other practice so seriously threatens our sport.

- **PARK IN DESIGNATED AREAS,** not in undeveloped, vegetated areas. Carpool to the crags!

- **MAINTAIN A LOW PROFILE.** Other people have the same right to undisturbed enjoyment of natural areas as do you.

- **RESPECT PRIVATE PROPERTY.** Don't trespass in order to climb.

- **JOIN OR FORM A GROUP TO DEAL WITH ACCESS ISSUES IN YOUR AREA.** Consider clean-ups, trail building or maintenance, or other "goodwill" projects.

- **JOIN THE ACCESS FUND.** To become a member, *simply make a donation (tax-deductible) of any amount.* Only by working together can we preserve the diverse American climbing experience.

The Access Fund. Preserving America's diverse climbing resources.
The Access Fund • P.O. Box 17010 • Boulder, CO 80308